SONGS

Of

INNOCENCE

and *Of*

EXPERIENCE

Shewing the Two Contrary States
of the Human Soul

1789 · 1794

The Author & Printer W Blake

Oxford University Press, Walton Street, Oxford OX2 6DP

Oxford New York Toronto
Delhi Bombay Calcutta Madras Karachi
Petaling Jaya Singapore Hong Kong Tokyo
Nairobi Dar es Salaam Cape Town
Melbourne Auckland

and associated companies in
Berlin Ibadan

Oxford is a trade mark of Oxford University Press

ISBN 0–19–281089–8

© The Trianon Press 1967

First published in 1967 by Rupert Hart-Davis Ltd.
and by The Orion Press, New York
in association with The Trianon Press
125 avenue du Marine, Paris 14e
First issued as an Oxford University Press paperback 1970
Reprinted 1977, 1982, 1984, 1985, 1986, 1987, 1988, 1989 (twice), 1990,
1991

The text was set in Monotype Caslon Old Face by
Spottiswoode, Ballantyne & Co. Ltd, London & Colchester
The book was designed by Arnold Fawcus

The title-page overleaf combines elements
from Blake's own title-pages, including
the dates of the 'Songs of Innocence' and
'Songs of Experience' respectively

Printed in Hong Kong

This reproduction in the original size

of William Blake's Illuminated Book

SONGS of INNOCENCE

AND OF

EXPERIENCE

with an Introduction and Commentary

by Sir Geoffrey Keynes

is published by

OXFORD UNIVERSITY PRESS

OXFORD & NEW YORK

in association with The Trianon Press, Paris

Contents

The text of each poem is given in letterpress on the verso of Blake's Illuminated Plates. The Commentary by Sir Geoffrey Keynes follows at the end of the volume.

Publisher's Note

The present volume has evolved from the publications of the William Blake Trust, to whom the publishers are greatly indebted. The hand-coloured Trust facsimile of *Songs of Innocence and of Experience*, made in 1955 and published in a very limited edition, has been out of print for some time now, and we have become increasingly aware of the need to make these poems, some of the finest and best-loved in the English language, accessible to a wider public in the form in which Blake intended them to be read.

The publishers are particularly grateful for his encouragement and advice to Mr. Lessing J. Rosenwald, whose original book, now in the Rosenwald Collection at the Library of Congress, served as the basis for this reproduction and to Sir Geoffrey Keynes, Chairman of the Blake Trust, without whose support this publication would not have been possible.

In the titles to the poems that are printed in letterpress on the verso of the colour plates, we have followed Blake's unconventional use of capitals, which was often guided by other than aesthetic considerations. These variations have not been observed either in the list of plates or in the Commentary; the latter, however, includes the text appearing on the three title-pages as Blake wrote it. In the poems Blake's punctuation has been followed as faithfully as possible, although his dot or 'breathing stop' has been translated into the more customary comma where this seemed indicated by the sense.

ARNOLD FAWCUS

Trianon Press, Paris

Introduction

WILLIAM BLAKE was born on 28 November 1757 into a world unready to receive the artist and poet of genius that he proved to be. His father was a hosier living in Broad Street in the Soho district of London. He was the second son of a family of four boys and one girl. Only his younger brother Robert was of great significance in William's life, as he was the one to share his devotion to the arts.

William very soon declared his intention of becoming an artist and was allowed to leave ordinary school at the age of ten to join a drawing school. Here he worked for five years, but, when the time came for an apprenticeship, his father was unable to afford the expense of his entrance to a painter's studio. A premium of fifty guineas, however, enabled him, aged nearly fifteen, to enter on 4 August 1772 the workshop of a master-engraver, James Basire. There, in Great Queen Street, Lincoln's Inn Fields, he worked faithfully for seven years, learning all the techniques of engraving, etching, stippling and copying. This thorough training equipped him as a man who could later claim with justice that he was one of the finest craftsmen of his time, one moreover able not only to develop and improve the conventional modes throughout his life, but also to invent methods of his own.

Having left school at ten years old he might be supposed to have neglected all further general education and reading, but his intellect developed early.

He became a voracious reader and by the age of twelve was writing poetry; this shewed, perhaps, the influence of some contemporary writers, but was nevertheless of great distinction and originality. In 1783 his friends paid for the printing of *Poetical Sketches*, a volume of verse written between the ages of twelve and twenty. This is now recognized as one of the major poetical events of the late eighteenth century, even Blake's *juvenilia* placing him among the chief initiators of the so-called 'romantic revival'.

Having emerged from his apprenticeship in 1779, a strongly built, lively young man, full of confidence in his own capacities, Blake entered as a student at the Royal Academy. He made drawings from the antique in the conventional manner and some life studies, though he soon rejected this form of training, saying that 'copying nature' deadened the force of his imagination. For the rest of his life he exalted imaginative art above all other forms of artistic creation, scarcely any of his productions being strictly representational. His art was in fact far too adventurous and unconventional to be easily accepted in the late eighteenth and early nineteenth centuries. For this reason Blake remained virtually unknown until Alexander Gilchrist's biography was published in 1863, and he was not fully accepted until his remarkable modernity and his imaginative force, both as poet and artist, were recognized in the twentieth century.

Blake was therefore obliged to earn his bread and butter for many years by working as a journeyman engraver, making engraved book-illustrations from designs by his more conventional, and therefore more successful, contemporaries, such as Stothard, Flaxman and Fuseli. By his twenty-fifth year Blake felt able to support a wife, and on 18 August 1782 married Catherine Boucher, the uneducated daughter of a Battersea market gardener. Lack of literacy did not prevent Mrs. Blake from proving to be an ideal wife for so unworldly an artist as William, learning to paint and draw until able to take part in his artistic output. Her only shortcoming, it would seem, was her inability to provide her husband with the children he would have delighted to raise.

Having married, Blake left his father's home and rented a small house round the corner in Poland Street, being joined there by his brother Robert after their father's death in 1784. William then began to train Robert as an artist. Meanwhile he himself, self-educated, had already acquired a wide knowledge of poetry, philosophy and general literature, and was ready to take his place among people of intelligence. He attended social gatherings of intellectuals, to whom he even communicated his own poems, sometimes singing them to tunes of his own composition. His mind was developing an unconventional and rebellious quality, acutely conscious of any falsity and pomposity in others, so that about 1784 he wrote a burlesque novel, known as *An Island in the Moon*, in which he ridiculed contemporary manners and conventions, not sparing himself. The manuscript of part of this *jeu d'esprit* has survived and has proved to contain, scattered among its absurdities, several of the poems afterwards known as *Songs of Innocence*. Having begun in this way, Blake recognized that these poems, so lightly thrown off, were better than their context, and about 1788 began to assemble a collection of them fit to be made into a small volume.

9

By this date Blake had become fully aware that he was the complete artist. He knew that poetry and design are the same thing in different forms, and he possessed the originality and craftsmanship needed for the practice of both, separately or simultaneously. He was not content, therefore, to see his poems only in a written form or in ordinary print as were his earlier *Poetical Sketches*. He wished to have them clothed in design and colour, so that each poem-picture formed an artistic whole. Meanwhile his beloved young brother, Robert, his companion and budding fellow-artist for a few happy years, had fallen seriously ill, and early in 1787 had died. William nursed him so assiduously that he is said to have gone without sleep for a fortnight, his exhaustion being so extreme after his brother's death that he slept continuously for three days and nights. At the moment of Robert's death his visionary faculty enabled him to see 'the released spirit ascend heavenwards, clapping its hands for joy'. For the rest of his life William claimed that he could communicate with his brother's spirit and gain strength from his advice.

This faculty was of special service in 1788-9, when Blake was puzzling over the problem of how to produce his poems in a form that satisfied him. A friend of his boyhood recorded in later years that Blake, in his perplexity, saw his brother before him in one of his imaginative visions. Robert's spirit then instructed him in how he should proceed, with the result that he quickly evolved his peculiar method of etching both poem and design in relief on a copper-plate; perfecting the means of doing this cost him endless labour, but it preserved his integrity as an artist.

Blake's method demanded the laborious transfer of a written text to an etched copper-plate, from which an impression could be printed in ink of any colour that he chose. The text would then be combined on the copper with illustrations or simple decorations harmonizing with the script, after which the whole print was coloured with pen or paint-brush, varied as he pleased in each copy that he made. Blake had found the means of presenting the written word to his readers as part of a picture, and once he had decided on this principle he had no thought of mass production, his method being far too slow.

After executing some small experimental plates in 1788, Blake made the twenty-seven plates of *Songs of Innocence*, dating the title-page 1789, and thus initiated the series of his now famous Illuminated Books. The impulse to produce his poems in this form was partly due to his cast of mind, whereby the life of the imagination was more real to him than the material world. This philosophy demanded the identification of ideas with symbols which could be translated into visual images, word and symbol each reinforcing the other. His lyrical poems have content enough to make them acceptable without the visual addition, but he did not choose that they should be read in this plain shape, and consequently his output of books reckoned in numbers of copies was always very limited.

Having made his early copies of *Songs of Innocence* with very simple colouring, Blake soon began to elaborate both theme and method. He was rapidly developing a philosophical system expressed in symbols of increasing complexity at the same time that he invented a method of printing his plates in colours, using pigments of unknown composition. Soon after completing his *Songs of Innocence* he composed an allegorical poem in irregular metre called *The Book of Thel*, colouring the prints as before with water-colour washes. The next work, known as *The Marriage of Heaven and Hell*, was written mostly in prose and the plates were done at first by the colour-printing method. About 1789 Blake and his wife had moved to a small house on the south side of the Thames in a terrace called Hercules Buildings, Lambeth. Here he set about making a number of books embodying his philosophical system which he expressed in an increasingly obscure form. These have become known as his Prophetic Books, their production going on at the same time as he was painting numbers of pictures and making large colour prints, using a tempera medium instead of oil paints for the former. With these we are not now concerned as they are not directly related to his poetry; this, however, was being affected by his increasing awareness of the social injustices of his time which directed his thoughts to the composition of a series of lyrical poems forming the sequence known as *Songs of Experience*. There is no reason for thinking that when he composed the *Songs of Innocence* he had already envisaged a second set of antithetical poems embodying *Experience*. The *Innocence* poems were the products of a mind in a state of innocence and of an imagination unspoiled by stains of worldliness. Public events and private emotions soon converted Innocence into Experience, producing Blake's preoccupation with the problem of Good and Evil. This, with his feelings of indignation and pity for the sufferings of mankind as he saw them in the streets of London, resulted in his composing the second set.

After executing some of the *Experience* plates by his colour-printing method, he reverted to the use of water-colour washes for these as for the first series. The title-page of *Songs of Experience* is dated 1794 and it is believed that he did not issue any separate copies of these poems, always combining them with the *Songs of Innocence* in a single volume, 'Shewing', as he asserted on the general title-page, 'the two Contrary States of the Human Soul'. The character of the designs for *Experience* is noticeably more severe than it is in those of *Innocence*, where the outlines are sometimes softened by additional engraved lines and the decorations given a more delicate beauty.

When he decided to issue the poems in a combined series, Blake made some rearrangements, transferring a few poems from *Innocence* to *Experience*, and varied the order of the plates in successive copies of the book. He even composed one poem, 'A Divine Image', and etched a plate for it, but never used it in any copy of the book. It is known only in an uncoloured print, which is reproduced here at the end of the sequence. He continued to colour sets of the prints as they were commissioned by his customers until near the time of his death in 1827. The later copies were more elaborately coloured and the arrangement became standardized from 1815 onwards. The present reproduction has been made from one of the latest of these, now in the Lessing J. Rosenwald Collection in the Library of Congress, Washington, D.C. It was bought from Blake by his friend, Henry Crabb Robinson, for five guineas in 1826. Only twenty-six other copies of the book are now known, and not all of these have the complete set of fifty-four plates. Yet even this small number shews Blake's *Songs* to have been the most popular of his Illuminated Books, the others being too unusual and too difficult to understand to attract many customers. He had to live mainly by his work as painter and engraver rather than by his output of poetry.

As Blake's writings came to be more widely appreciated than they had been during his lifetime, they appeared more and more often on ordinary printed pages. Many readers realized that Blake had not intended his poems to be read in this form, and have demanded something better, but the technical difficulty of attempting to reproduce them adequately in their original colours would have raised the cost to a prohibitive level. Only recently have technical advances made it possible to provide a relatively inexpensive reproduction of Blake's plates in a way approximating to what he himself would have approved.

Yet Blake's etched copper-plates when printed on his own hand-press did not always present a text that was easy to read. The more customary typographical reprint has therefore been placed here opposite each coloured plate and has not been in any way edited, but follows the text exactly as Blake etched it, with his perfunctory punctuation and sometimes peculiar spelling. It is assumed that all readers will be grateful for this. It is not certain, however, that every reader will wish for an editor's commentary on both poems and designs, so that the brief explanation has been placed after each plate and can be ignored. It is nevertheless probable that many readers will find these tentative explanations useful. They have deliberately been made short, even superficial, not pretending to be complete expositions of Blake's thought and meaning.

They are intended only to suggest clues to the understanding of poems and designs so that the reader can build on them for himself or reject them in favour of better explanations of his own.

The philosophy and symbols of Blake's *Songs* have exercised the minds of many commentators. The first systematic study will be found in Joseph Wicksteed's *Blake's Innocence and Experience*, published in 1928. Readers wanting more illumination are recommended, after reading Gilchrist's *Life* (1863, and many times reprinted) and David Erdman's *Prophet against Empire* (1954), to study Wicksteed's book reinforced by S. Foster Damon's *Blake's Philosophy and Symbols* (1924), the same author's *Blake Dictionary* (1965), and E. D. Hirsch, Jr.'s *Introduction to Blake* (1964). Every book on Blake, biographical, critical or exegetical, necessarily gives some attention to the *Songs of Innocence and of Experience*, since they are basic to the understanding of Blake's mind.

GEOFFREY KEYNES

SONGS Of INNOCENCE
and Of EXPERIENCE

Shewing the Two Contrary States of the Human Soul

Frontispiece to *Songs of Innocence*

SONGS of Innocence

1789

The Author & Printer W Blake

Introduction

Piping down the valleys wild
Piping songs of pleasant glee
On a cloud I saw a child.
And he laughing said to me.

Pipe a song about a Lamb:
So I piped with merry chear,
Piper pipe that song again—
So I piped, he wept to hear.

Drop thy pipe thy happy pipe
Sing thy songs of happy chear,
So I sung the same again
While he wept with joy to hear.

Piper sit thee down and write
In a book that all may read—
So he vanish'd from my sight,
And I pluck'd a hollow reed.

And I made a rural pen,
And I stain'd the water clear,
And I wrote my happy songs,
Every child may joy to hear

Introduction

Piping down the valleys wild
Piping songs of pleasant glee
On a cloud I saw a child.
And he laughing said to me

Pipe a song about a Lamb;
So I piped with merry chear,
Piper pipe that song again
So I piped he wept to hear.

Drop thy pipe thy happy pipe
Sing thy songs of happy chear
So I sung the same again
While he wept with joy to hear

Piper sit thee down and write
In a book that all may read
So he vanish'd from my sight
And I pluck'd a hollow reed

And I made a rural pen,
And I stain'd the water clear
And I wrote my happy songs
Every child may joy to hear

The Shepherd.

How sweet is the Shepherds sweet lot,
From the morn to the evening he strays;
He shall follow his sheep all the day,
And his tongue shall be filled with praise.

For he hears the lambs innocent call,
And he hears the ewes tender reply;
He is watchful while they are in peace,
For they know when their Shepherd is nigh.

The Shepherd.

How sweet is the Shepherds sweet lot,
From the morn to the evening he strays:
He shall follow his sheep all the day
And his tongue shall be filled with praise.

For he hears the lambs innocent call.
And he hears the ewes tender reply.
He is watchful while they are in peace,
For they know when their Shepherd is nigh.

The Ecchoing Green

The Sun does arise,
And make happy the skies.
The merry bells ring,
To welcome the Spring.
The sky-lark and thrush,
The birds of the bush,
Sing louder around,
To the bells chearful sound,
While our sports shall be seen
On the Ecchoing Green.

Old John with white hair
Does laugh away care,
Sitting under the oak,
Among the old folk.

They

The Echoing Green

The Sun does arise,
And make happy the skies,
The merry bells ring
To welcome the Spring,
The sky-lark and thrush,
The birds of the bush,
Sing louder around
To the bells cheerful sound,
While our sports shall be seen
On the Echoing Green.

Old John with white hair
Does laugh away care,
Sitting under the oak,
Among the old folk.

They laugh at our play,
And soon they all say
Such such were the joys.
When we all girls & boys.
In our youth time were seen.
On the Echoing Green.

Till the little ones weary
No more can be merry
The sun does descend.
And our sports have an end:
Round the laps of their mothers
Many sisters and brothers
Like birds in their nest.
Are ready for rest:
And sport no more seen,
On the darkening Green.

They laugh at our play,
And soon they all say,
Such such were the joys,
When we all girls & boys,
In our youth time were seen,
On the Ecchoing Green.

Till the little ones weary
No more can be merry
The sun does descend,
And our sports have an end:
Round the laps of their mothers,
Many sisters and brothers,
Like birds in their nest,
Are ready for rest:
And sport no more seen,
On the darkening Green.

The Lamb

Little Lamb who made thee
  Dost thou know who made thee
Gave thee life & bid thee feed,
By the stream & o'er the mead;
Gave thee clothing of delight,
Softest clothing wooly bright;
Gave thee such a tender voice,
Making all the vales rejoice:
  Little Lamb who made thee
  Dost thou know who made thee

  Little Lamb I'll tell thee,
  Little Lamb Ill tell thee;
He is called by thy name,
For he calls himself a Lamb:
He is meek & he is mild,
He became a little child:
I a child & thou a lamb,
We are called by his name.
  Little Lamb God bless thee,
  Little Lamb God bless thee.

The Lamb

Little Lamb who made thee
Dost thou know who made thee
Gave thee life & bid thee feed.
By the stream & o'er the mead;
Gave thee clothing of delight,
Softest clothing wooly bright;
Gave thee such a tender voice,
Making all the vales rejoice!
    Little Lamb who made thee
    Dost thou know who made thee

Little Lamb I'll tell thee,
Little Lamb I'll tell thee!
He is called by thy name
For he calls himself a Lamb:
He is meek & he is mild,
He became a little child:
I a child & thou a lamb,
We are called by his name.
    Little Lamb God bless thee.
    Little Lamb God bless thee.

The Little Black Boy

My mother bore me in the southern wild,
And I am black, but O! my soul is white
White as an angel is the English child:
But I am black as if bereav'd of light.

My mother taught me underneath a tree
And sitting down before the heat of day
She took me on her lap and kissed me.
And pointing to the east began to say.

Look on the rising sun: there God does live
And gives his light, and gives his heat away.
And flowers and trees and beasts and men reciev
Comfort in morning joy in the noon day.

And we are put on earth a little space,
That we may learn to bear the beams of love.
And these black bodies and this sun-burnt face
Is but a cloud and like a shady grove.

For

The Little Black Boy.

My mother bore me in the southern wild,
And I am black, but O! my soul is white,
White as an angel is the English child:
But I am black as if bereav'd of light.

My mother taught me underneath a tree
And sitting down before the heat of day,
She took me on her lap and kissed me,
And pointing to the east began to say.

Look on the rising sun: there God does live
And gives his light, and gives his heat away.
And flowers and trees and beasts and men recieve
Comfort in morning joy in the noon day.

And we are put on earth a little space,
That we may learn to bear the beams of love.
And these black bodies and this sun-burnt face
Is but a cloud, and like a shady grove.

For

For when our souls have learn'd the heat to bear
The cloud will vanish we shall hear his voice,
Saying: come out from the grove my love & care,
And round my golden tent like lambs rejoice.

Thus did my mother say and kissed me.
And thus I say to little English boy.
When I from black and he from white cloud free,
And round the tent of God like lambs we joy:

Ill shade him from the heat till he can bear,
To lean in joy upon our fathers knee.
And then I'll stand and stroke his silver hair,
And be like him and he will then love me.

For when our souls have learn'd the heat to bear
The cloud will vanish we shall hear his voice.
Saying: come out from the grove my love & care.
And round my golden tent like lambs rejoice.

Thus did my mother say and kissed me.
And thus I say to little English boy.
When I from black and he from white cloud free,
And round the tent of God like lambs we joy:

I'll shade him from the heat till he can bear,
To lean in joy upon our fathers knee.
And then I'll stand and stroke his silver hair,
And be like him and he will then love me.

The Blossom.

Merry Merry Sparrow
Under leaves so green
A happy Blossom
Sees you swift as arrow
Seek your cradle narrow
Near my Bosom.

Pretty Pretty Robin
Under leaves so green
A happy Blossom
Hears you sobbing sobbing
Pretty Pretty Robin
Near my Bosom.

The Blossom.

Merry Merry Sparrow
Under leaves so green
A happy Blossom
Sees you swift as arrow
Seek your cradle narrow
Near my Bosom.

Pretty Pretty Robin
Under leaves so green
A happy Blossom
Hears you sobbing sobbing
Pretty Pretty Robin
Near my Bosom.

The Chimney Sweeper

When my mother died I was very young,
And my father sold me while yet my tongue,
Could scarcely cry weep weep weep weep.
So your chimneys I sweep & in soot I sleep.

Theres little Tom Dacre, who cried when his head
That curl'd like a lambs back, was shav'd, so I said,
Hush Tom never mind it, for when your head's bare,
You know that the soot cannot spoil your white hair.

And so he was quiet, & that very night,
As Tom was a sleeping he had such a sight,
That thousands of sweepers Dick, Joe, Ned & Jack
Were all of them lock'd up in coffins of black,

And by came an Angel who had a bright key,
And he open'd the coffins & set them all free.
Then down a green plain leaping laughing they run
And wash in a river and shine in the Sun.

Then naked & white, all their bags left behind,
They rise upon clouds, and sport in the wind.
And the Angel told Tom, if he'd be a good boy,
He'd have God for his father & never want joy.

And so Tom awoke and we rose in the dark
And got with our bags & our brushes to work.
Tho' the morning was cold, Tom was happy & warm.
So if all do their duty, they need not fear harm.

The Chimney Sweeper

When my mother died I was very young,
And my father sold me while yet my tongue,
Could scarcely cry weep weep weep weep.
So your chimneys I sweep & in soot I sleep.

Theres little Tom Dacre, who cried when his head
That curld like a lambs back, was shav'd, so I said,
Hush Tom never mind it, for when your heads bare,
You know that the soot cannot spoil your white hair

And so he was quiet, & that very night,
As Tom was a sleeping he had such a sight,
That thousands of sweepers Dick, Joe Ned & Jack
Were all of them lock'd up in coffins of black,

And by came an Angel who had a bright key,
And he open'd the coffins & set them all free.
Then down a green plain leaping laughing they run
And wash in a river and shine in the Sun.

Then naked & white, all their bags left behind,
They rise upon clouds, and sport in the wind.
And the Angel told Tom if he'd be a good boy,
He'd have God for his father & never want joy.

And so Tom awoke and we rose in the dark
And got with our bags & our brushes to work.
Tho' the morning was cold, Tom was happy & warm,
So if all do their duty, they need not fear harm.

The Little Boy lost

Father, father where are you going
O do not walk so fast.
Speak father, speak to your little boy
Or else I shall be lost.

The night was dark no father was there
The child was wet with dew.
The mire was deep, & the child did weep
And away the vapour flew

The Little Boy lost

Father, father, where are you going
O do not walk so fast.
Speak father, speak to your little boy
Or else I shall be lost,

The night was dark no father was there
The child was wet with dew.
The mire was deep, & the child did weep
And away the vapour flew.

The Little Boy found

The little boy lost in the lonely fen,
Led by the wand'ring light,
Began to cry, but God ever nigh,
Appeard like his father in white.

He kissed the child & by the hand led
And to his mother brought,
Who in sorrow pale, thro' the lonely dale
Her little boy weeping sought.

The Little Boy found

The little boy lost in the lonely fen,
Led by the wandring light,
Began to cry, but God ever nigh,
Appeard like his father in white.

He kissed the child & by the hand led
And to his mother brought,
Who in sorrow pale, thro' the lonely dale
Her little boy weeping sought.

Laughing Song

When the green woods laugh with the voice of joy
And the dimpling stream runs laughing by,
When the air does laugh with our merry wit,
And the green hill laughs with the noise of it.

When the meadows laugh with lively green
And the grasshopper laughs in the merry scene,
When Mary and Susan and Emily,
With their sweet round mouths sing Ha, Ha, He.

When the painted birds laugh in the shade
Where our table with cherries and nuts is spread
Come live & be merry and join with me,
To sing the sweet chorus of Ha, Ha, He.

Laughing Song,

When the green woods laugh with the voice of joy
And the dimpling stream runs laughing by,
When the air does laugh with our merry wit,
And the green hill laughs with the noise of it.

When the meadows laugh with lively green
And the grasshopper laughs in the merry scene,
When Mary and Susan and Emily,
With their sweet round mouths sing Ha, Ha, He.

When the painted birds laugh in the shade
Where our table with cherries and nuts is spread
Come live & be merry and join with me,
To sing the sweet chorus of Ha, Ha, He.

A Cradle song

Sweet dreams form a shade,
O'er my lovely infants head.
Sweet dreams of pleasant streams,
By happy silent moony beams

Sweet sleep with soft down,
Weave thy brows an infant crown.
Sweet sleep Angel mild,
Hover o'er my happy child.

Sweet smiles in the night,
Hover over my delight.
Sweet smiles Mothers smiles
All the livelong night beguiles.

Sweet moans, dovelike sighs,
Chase not slumber from thy eyes,
Sweet moans, sweeter smiles,
All the dovelike moans beguiles.

Sleep sleep happy child.
All creation slept and smil'd.
Sleep sleep, happy sleep,
While o'er thee thy mother weep

Sweet babe in thy face,
Holy image I can trace.
Sweet babe once like thee,
Thy maker lay and wept for me

Wept

A CRADLE SONG

Sweet dreams form a shade
O'er my lovely infants head.
Sweet dreams of pleasant streams.
By happy silent moony beams

Sweet sleep with soft down.
Weave thy brows an infant crown.
Sweet sleep Angel mild,
Hover o'er my happy child.

Sweet smiles in the night,
Hover over my delight.
Sweet smiles Mothers smiles
All the livelong night beguiles.

Sweet moans, dovelike sighs,
Chase not slumber from thy eyes,
Sweet moans, sweeter smiles,
All the dovelike moans beguiles.

Sleep sleep happy child,
All creation slept and smild.
Sleep sleep, happy sleep,
While o'er thee thy mother weep

Sweet babe in thy face,
Holy image I can trace.
Sweet babe once like thee,
Thy maker lay and wept for me

Wept for me for thee for all.
When he was an infant small.
Thou his image ever see.
Heavenly face that smiles on thee.

Smiles on thee on me on all
Who became an infant small.
Infant smiles are his own smiles.
Heaven & earth to peace beguiles.

Wept for me for thee for all,
When he was an infant small.
Thou his image ever see.
Heavenly face that smiles on thee.

Smiles on thee on me on all,
Who became an infant small,
Infant smiles are his own smiles,
Heaven & earth to peace beguiles.

The Divine Image.

To Mercy Pity Peace and Love,
All pray in their distress:
And to these virtues of delight
Return their thankfulness.

For Mercy Pity Peace and Love,
Is God our father dear:
And Mercy Pity Peace and Love,
Is Man his child and care.

For Mercy has a human heart
Pity, a human face:
And Love, the human form divine,
And Peace, the human dress.

Then every man of every clime,
That prays in his distress,
Prays to the human form divine
Love Mercy Pity Peace.

And all must love the human form,
In heathen, turk or jew.
Where Mercy, Love & Pity dwell,
There God is dwelling too.

The Divine Image.

To Mercy Pity Peace and Love,
All pray in their distress;
And to these virtues of delight
Return their thankfulness.

For Mercy Pity Peace and Love,
Is God our father dear;
And Mercy Pity Peace and Love,
Is Man his child and care.

For Mercy has a human heart,
Pity, a human face;
And Love, the human form divine,
And Peace, the human dress.

Then every man of every clime,
That prays in his distress,
Prays to the human form divine
Love Mercy Pity Peace.

And all must love the human form,
In heathen, turk or jew,
Where Mercy, Love & Pity dwell
There God is dwelling too.

HOLY THURSDAY

Twas on a Holy Thursday their innocent faces clean
The children walking two & two in red & blue & green
Grey headed beadles walkd before with wands as white as snow
Till into the high dome of Pauls they like Thames waters flow

O what a multitude they seemd these flowers of London town
Seated in companies they sit with radiance all their own
The hum of multitudes was there but multitudes of lambs
Thousands of little boys & girls raising their innocent hands

Now like a mighty wind they raise to heaven the voice of song
Or like harmonious thunderings the seats of heaven among
Beneath them sit the aged men wise guardians of the poor
Then cherish pity, lest you drive an angel from your door

HOLY THURSDAY

Twas on a Holy Thursday their innocent faces clean
The children walking two & two in red & blue & green
Grey headed beadles walkd before with wands as white as snow
Till into the high dome of Pauls they like Thames waters flow

O what a multitude they seemd these flowers of London town
Seated in companies they sit with radiance all their own
The hum of multitudes was there but multitudes of lambs
Thousands of little boys & girls raising their innocent hands

Now like a mighty wind they raise to heaven the voice of song
Or like harmonious thunderings the seats of heaven among
Beneath them sit the aged men wise guardians of the poor
Then cherish pity; lest you drive an angel from your door

Night

The sun descending in the west,
The evening star does shine,
The birds are silent in their nest,
And I must seek for mine,
The moon like a flower,
In heavens high bower;
With silent delight,
Sits and smiles on the night.

Farewell green fields and happy groves,
Where flocks have took delight;
Where lambs have nibbled, silent moves
The feet of angels bright;
Unseen they pour blessing,
And joy without ceasing,
On each bud and blossom,
And each sleeping bosom.

They look in every thoughtless nest,
Where birds are coverd warm;
They visit caves of every beast,
To keep them all from harm:
If they see any weeping,
That should have been sleeping
They pour sleep on their head
And sit down by their bed.

When

Night

The sun descending in the west,
The evening star does shine.
The birds are silent in their nest.
And I must seek for mine
The moon like a flower.
In heavens high bower,
With silent delight.
Sits and smiles on the night.

Farewell green fields and happy groves.
Where flocks have took delight;
Where lambs have nibbled, silent moves
The feet of angels bright;
Unseen they pour blessing,
And joy without ceasing.
On each bud and blossom,
And each sleeping bosom.

They look in every thoughtless nest.
Where birds are coverd warm;
They visit caves of every beast,
To keep them all from harm:
If they see any weeping,
That should have been sleeping,
They pour sleep on their head
And sit down by their bed.

When wolves and tygers howl for prey
They pitying stand and weep;
Seeking to drive their thirst away,
And keep them from the sheep.
But if they rush dreadful,
The angels most heedful,
Receive each mild spirit,
New worlds to inherit.

And there the lions ruddy eyes,
Shall flow with tears of gold:
And pitying the tender cries,
And walking round the fold:
Saying: wrath by his meekness
And by his health, sickness,
Is driven away,
From our immortal day.

And now beside thee bleating lamb,
I can lie down and sleep;
Or think on him who bore thy name,
Grase after thee and weep.
For wash'd in lifes river,
My bright mane for ever,
Shall shine like the gold,
As I guard o'er the fold

When wolves and tygers howl for prey
They pitying stand and weep;
Seeking to drive their thirst away,
And keep them from the sheep,
But if they rush dreadful;
The angels most heedful,
Recieve each mild spirit,
New worlds to inherit.

And there the lions ruddy eyes,
Shall flow with tears of gold:
And pitying the tender cries,
And walking round the fold:
Saying: wrath by his meekness
And by his health, sickness,
Is driven away,
From our immortal day.

And now beside thee bleating lamb,
I can lie down and sleep;
Or think on him who bore thy name,
Grase after thee and weep.
For wash'd in lifes river,
My bright mane for ever,
Shall shine like the gold,
As I guard o'er the fold.

Spring

Sound the Flute!
Now it's mute.
Birds delight
Day and Night.
Nightingale
In the dale
Lark in Sky
Merrily
Merrily Merrily to welcome in the Year

Little Boy
Full of joy.

Little

Spring

Sound the Flute!
Now it's mute.
Birds delight
Day and Night.
Nightingale
In the dale
Lark in Sky
Merrily
Merrily Merrily to welcome in the (Year

Little Boy
Full of joy.
                                    Little

Little Girl
Sweet and small.
Cock does crow
So do you.
Merry voice
Infant noise
Merrily Merrily to welcome in the Year.

Little Lamb
Here I am
Come and lick
My white neck.
Let me pull
Your soft Wool.
Let me kiss
Your soft face.
Merrily Merrily we welcome in the Year

Little Girl
Sweet and small.
Cock does crow
So do you.
Merry voice
Infant noise
Merrily Merrily to welcome in the Year

Little Lamb
Here I am,
Come and lick
My white neck.
Let me pull
Your soft Wool.
Let me kiss
Your soft face.
Merrily Merrily we welcome in the Year

Nurse's Song

When the voices of children are heard on the green
And laughing is heard on the hill,
My heart is at rest within my breast
And everything else is still

Then come home my children, the sun is gone down
And the dews of night arise
Come come leave off play, and let us away
Till the morning appears in the skies

No no let us play, for it is yet day
And we cannot go to sleep
Besides in the sky, the little birds fly
And the hills are all coverd with sheep

Well well go & play till the light fades away
And then go home to bed
The little ones leaped & shouted & laugh'd
And all the hills ecchoed

Nurses Song

When the voices of children are heard on the green
And laughing is heard on the hill
My heart is at rest within my breast
And every thing else is still

Then come home my children the sun is gone down
And the dews of night arise
Come come leave off play, and let us away
Till the morning appears in the skies

No no let us play, for it is yet day
And we cannot go to sleep
Besides in the sky, the little birds fly
And the hills are all coverd with sheep

Well well go & play till the light fades away
And then go home to bed
The little ones leaped & shouted & laugh'd
And all the hills echoed

Infant Joy

I have no name
I am but two days old
What shall I call thee? —
I happy am
Joy is my name —
Sweet joy befall thee!

Pretty joy!
Sweet joy but two days old.
Sweet joy I call thee:
Thou dost smile,
I sing the while
Sweet joy befall thee.

Infant Joy

I have no name
I am but two days old.—
What shall I call thee?
I happy am
Joy is my name,—
Sweet joy befall thee!

Pretty joy!
Sweet joy but two days old.
Sweet joy I call thee:
Thou dost smile.
I sing the while
Sweet joy befall thee.

A Dream

Once a dream did weave a shade,
O'er my Angel-guarded bed,
That an Emmet lost it's way
Where on grass methought I lay.

Troubled wilderd and folorn
Dark benighted travel-worn,
Over many a tangled spray,
All heart-broke I heard her say.

O my children! do they cry,
Do they hear their father sigh.
Now they look abroad to see,
Now return and weep for me.

Pitying I drop'd a tear:
But I saw a glow-worm near:
Who replied, What wailing wight
Calls the watchman of the night.

I am set to light the ground,
While the beetle goes his round:
Follow now the beetles hum,
Little wanderer hie thee home.

A Dream

Once a dream did weave a shade.
O'er my Angel-guarded bed.
That an Emmet lost its way
Where on grass methought I lay.

Troubled wilderd and forlorn
Dark benighted travel-worn.
Over many a tangled spray
All heart-broke I heard her say

O my children! do they cry.
Do they hear their father sigh.
Now they look abroad to see.
Now return and weep for me.

Pitying I dropd a tear:
But I saw a glow-worm near:
Who replied. What wailing wight
Calls the watchman of the night.

I am set to light the ground,
While the beetle goes his round:
Follow now the beetles hum,
Little wanderer hie thee home

On Anothers Sorrow

Can I see anothers woe,
And not be in sorrow too.
Can I see anothers grief
And not seek for kind relief.

Can I see a falling tear,
And not feel my sorrows share,
Can a father see his child
Weep, nor be with sorrow fill'd.

Can a mother sit and hear,
An infant groan an infant fear—
No no never can it be.
Never never can it be.

And can he who smiles on all
Hear the wren with sorrows small
Hear the small birds grief & care
Hear the woes that infants bear.

And not sit beside the nest
Pouring pity in their breast.
And not sit the cradle near
Weeping tear on infants tear.

And not sit both night & day.
Wiping all our tears away.
O! no never can it be.
Never never can it be.

He doth give his joy to all.
He becomes an infant small
He becomes a man of woe
He doth feel the sorrow too.

Think not, thou canst sigh a sigh,
And thy maker is not by.
Think not, thou canst weep a tear,
And thy maker is not near.

O! he gives to us his joy,
That our grief he may destroy
Till our grief is fled & gone
He doth sit by us and moan

On Anothers Sorrow

Can I see anothers woe,
And not be in sorrow too.
Can I see anothers grief,
And not seek for kind relief.

Can I see a falling tear,
And not feel my sorrows share,
Can a father see his child,
Weep, nor be with sorrow fill'd.

Can a mother sit and hear,
An infant groan an infant fear—
No no never can it be.
Never never can it be.

And can he who smiles on all
Hear the wren with sorrows small,
Hear the small birds grief & care
Hear the woes that infants bear—

And not sit beside the nest
Pouring pity in their breast.
And not sit the cradle near
Weeping tear on infants tear.

And not sit both night & day,
Wiping all our tears away.
O! no never can it be.
Never never can it be.

He doth give his joy to all.
He becomes an infant small.
He becomes a man of woe
He doth feel the sorrow too.

Think not, thou canst sigh a sigh,
And thy maker is not by.
Think not, thou canst weep a tear
And thy maker is not near.

O! he gives to us his joy,
That our grief he may destroy
Till our grief is fled & gone
He doth sit by us and moan

Frontispiece to *Songs of Experience*

SONGS
of
EXPERIENCE

The Author & Printer W Blake

SONGS of EXPERIENCE

1794

The Author & Printer W Blake

Introduction.

Hear the voice of the Bard!
Who Present, Past, & Future sees
Whose ears have heard,
The Holy Word,
That walk'd among the ancient trees.

Calling the lapsed Soul
And weeping in the evening dew:
That might controll
The starry pole:
And fallen fallen light renew!

O Earth O Earth return!
Arise from out the dewy grass;
Night is worn,
And the morn
Rises from the slumberous mass.

Turn away no more:
Why wilt thou turn away
The starry floor
The watry shore
Is giv'n thee till the break of day.

Introduction.

Hear the voice of the Bard!
Who, Present, Past, & Future sees
Whose ears have heard,
The Holy Word,
That walk'd among the ancient trees.

Calling the lapsed Soul
And weeping in the evening dew:
That might controll.
The starry pole;
And fallen fallen light renew!

O Earth O Earth return!
Arise from out the dewy grass;
Night is worn.
And the morn
Rises from the slumberous mass.

Turn away no more:
Why wilt thou turn away
The starry floor
The watry shore
Is giv'n thee till the break of day.

EARTH'S Answer

Earth rais'd up her head,
From the darkness dread & drear.
Her light fled,
Stony dread!
And her locks cover'd with grey despair.

Prison'd on watry shore
Starry Jealousy does keep my den
Cold and hoar
Weeping o'er
I hear the father of the ancient men

Selfish father of men
Cruel jealous selfish fear
Can delight
Chain'd in night
The virgins of youth and morning bear.

Does spring hide its joy
When buds and blossoms grow?
Does the sower?
Sow by night?
Or the plowman in darkness plow?

Break this heavy chain,
That does freeze my bones around
Selfish! vain!
Eternal bane!
That free Love with bondage bound.

EARTH'S Answer.

Earth rais'd up her head,
From the darkness dread & drear,
Her light fled:
Stony dread!
And her locks cover'd with grey despair.

Prison'd on watry shore
Starry Jealousy does keep my den
Cold and hoar
Weeping o'er
I hear the Father of the ancient men

Selfish father of men
Cruel jealous selfish fear
Can delight
Chain'd in night
The virgins of youth and morning bear.

Does spring hide its joy
When buds and blossoms grow?
Does the sower?
Sow by night?
Or the plowman in darkness plow?

Break this heavy chain,
That does freeze my bones around
Selfish! vain!
Eternal bane!
That free Love with bondage bound.

The CLOD & the PEBBLE

Love seeketh not Itself to please,
Nor for itself hath any care;
But for another gives its ease,
And builds a Heaven in Hells despair.

So sang a little Clod of Clay,
Trodden with the cattles feet;
But a Pebble of the brook,
Warbled out these metres meet.

Love seeketh only Self to please,
To bind another to Its delight:
Joys in anothers loss of ease,
And builds a Hell in Heavens despite.

The CLOD & the PEBBLE

Love seeketh not Itself to please,
Nor for itself hath any care;
But for another gives its ease,
And builds a Heaven in Hells despair.

So sang a little Clod of Clay
Trodden with the cattles feet:
But a Pebble of the brook,
Warbled out these metres meet.

Love seeketh only Self to please,
To bind another to its delight:
Joys in anothers loss of ease,
And builds a Hell in Heavens despite.

HOLY THURSDAY

Is this a holy thing to see,
In a rich and fruitful land
Babes reduced to misery,
Fed with cold and usurous hand?

Is that trembling cry a song?
Can it be a song of joy?
And so many children poor?
It is a land of poverty!

And their sun does never shine.
And their fields are bleak & bare.
And their ways are filld with thorns
It is eternal winter there

For where-eer the sun does shine.
And where-eer the rain does fall:
Babe can never hunger there,
Nor poverty the mind appall.

HOLY THURSDAY

Is this a holy thing to see,
In a rich and fruitful land,
Babes reducd to misery,
Fed with cold and usurous hand?

Is that trembling cry a song?
Can it be a song of joy?
And so many children poor?
It is a land of poverty!

And their sun does never shine.
And their fields are bleak & bare.
And their ways are fill'd with thorns
It is eternal winter there.

For where-e'er the sun does shine,
And where-e'er the rain does fall:
Babe can never hunger there,
Nor poverty the mind appall.

The Little Girl Lost

In futurity
I prophetic see,
That the earth from sleep,
(Grave the sentence deep)

Shall arise and seek
For her maker meek:
And the desart wild
Become a garden mild.

In the southern clime,
Where the summers prime,
Never fades away;
Lovely Lyca lay.

Seven summers old
Lovely Lyca told,
She had wanderd long,
Hearing wild birds song.

Sweet sleep come to me
Underneath this tree;
Do father, mother weep,—
"Where can Lyca sleep".

Lost in desart wild
Is your little child.
How can Lyca sleep,
If her mother weep.

If her heart does ake,
Then let Lyca wake;
If my mother sleep,
Lyca shall not weep.

Frowning frowning night,
O'er this desart bright,
Let thy moon arise,
While I close my eyes.

Sleeping Lyca lay;
While the beasts of prey,
Come from caverns deep,
View'd the maid asleep

The kingly lion stood
And the virgin view'd,
Then he gambold round
O'er the hallowd ground:

Leopards

The Little Girl Lost

In futurity
I prophetic see,
That the earth from sleep,
(Grave the sentence deep)

Shall arise and seek
For her maker meek:
And the desart wild
Become a garden mild.

In the southern clime,
Where the summers prime,
Never fades away;
Lovely Lyca lay.

Seven summers old
Lovely Lyca told.
She had wanderd long,
Hearing wild birds song.

Sweet sleep come to me
Underneath this tree;
Do father, mother weep.—
Where can Lyca sleep.

Lost in desart wild
Is your little child.
How can Lyca sleep,
If her mother weep.

If her heart does ake,
Then let Lyca wake;
If my mother sleep,
Lyca shall not weep.

Frowning frowning night,
O'er this desart bright,
Let thy moon arise,
While I close my eyes.

Sleeping Lyca lay;
While the beasts of prey,
Come from caverns deep,
View'd the maid asleep

The kingly lion stood
And the virgin view'd,
Then he gambold round
O'er the hallowd ground

Leopards, tygers play,
Round her as she lay;
While the lion old,
Bow'd his mane of gold,

And her bosom lick,
And upon her neck,
From his eyes of flame,
Ruby tears there came;

While the lioness
Loos'd her slender dress
And naked they convey'd
To caves the sleeping maid.

The Little Girl Found

All the night in woe,
Lyca's parents go:
Over vallies deep,
While the desarts weep.

Tired and woe begone,
Hoarse with making moan:
Arm in arm seven days,
They trac'd the desart ways.

Seven nights they sleep,
Among shadows deep:
And dream they see their child
Starv'd in desart wild.

Pale thro' pathless ways
The fancied image strays,

Leopards, tygers play,
Round her as she lay;
While the lion old,
Bow'd his mane of gold,

And her bosom lick,
And upon her neck,

From his eyes of flame,
Ruby tears there came;

While the lioness
Loos'd her slender dress,
And naked they convey'd
To caves the sleeping maid.

The Little Girl Found

All the night in woe,
Lyca's parents go:
Over vallies deep,
While the desarts weep.

Tired and woe-begone,
Hoarse with making moan:
Arm in arm seven days,
They trac'd the desart ways.

Seven nights they sleep,
Among shadows deep:
And dream they see their child
Starv'd in desart wild.

Pale thro' pathless ways
The fancied image strays,

Famish'd

Famish'd, weeping, weak
With hollow piteous shriek

Rising from unrest,
The trembling woman prest,
With feet of weary woe;
She could no further go.

In his arms he bore,
Her arm'd with sorrow sore:
Till before their way,
A couching lion lay.

Turning back was vain,
Soon his heavy mane,
Bore them to the ground;
Then he stalk'd around.

Smelling to his prey,
But their fears allay,
When he licks their hands:
And silent by them stands.

They look upon his eyes
Fill'd with deep surprise:
And wondering behold,
A spirit arm'd in gold.

On his head a crown
On his shoulders down,
Flow'd his golden hair.
Gone was all their care.

Follow me he said,
Weep not for the maid:
In my palace deep,
Lyca lies asleep.

Then they followed,
Where the vision led:
And saw their sleeping child,
Among tygers wild.

To this day they dwell
In a lonely dell
Nor fear the wolvish howl,
Nor the lions growl.

Lyca weeping weak,
With hollow piteous shriek

Rising from unrest,
The trembling woman prest
With feet of weary woe;
She could no further go

In his arms he bore
Her arm'd with sorrow sore
Till before their way
A couching lion lay

Turning back was vain,
Soon his heavy mane
Bore them to the ground;
Then he stalk'd around.

Smelling to his prey
But their fears allay,
When he licks their hands,
And silent by them stands.

They look upon his eyes
Fill'd with deep surprise
And wondering behold,
A Spirit arm'd in gold.

On his head a crown
On his shoulders down,
Flow'd his golden hair.
Gone was all their care.

Follow me he said,
Weep not for the maid;
In my pallace deep,
Lyca lies asleep.

Then they followed,
Where the vision led:
And saw their sleeping child
Among tygers wild.

To this day they dwell
In a lonely dell
Nor fear the wolvish howl,
Nor the lions growl.

The Chimney Sweeper

A little black thing among the snow:
Crying weep, weep, in notes of woe!
Where are thy father & mother? say?
They are both gone up to the church to pray.

Because I was happy upon the heath,
And smil'd among the winters snow:
They clothed me in the clothes of death,
And taught me to sing the notes of woe.

And because I am happy & dance & sing,
They think they have done me no injury:
And are gone to praise God & his Priest & King
Who make up a heaven of our misery.

The Chimney Sweeper

A little black thing among the snow:
Crying weep, weep, in notes of woe!
Where are thy father & mother? say?
They are both gone up to the church to pray.

Because I was happy upon the heath,
And smil'd among the winters snow:
They clothed me in the clothes of death,
And taught me to sing the notes of woe.

And because I am happy, & dance & sing,
They think they have done me no injury:
And are gone to praise God & his Priest & King
Who make up a heaven of our misery.

NURSES Song

When the voices of children, are heard on the green
And whisprings are in the dale:
The days of my youth rise fresh in my mind,
My face turns green and pale.

Then come home my children, the sun is gone down
And the dews of night arise
Your spring & your day, are wasted in play
And your winter and night in disguise.

NURSES Song

Where the voices of children are heard on the green
And whisperings are in the dale,
The days of my youth rise fresh in my mind,
My face turns green and pale.

Then come home my children, the sun is gone down
And the dews of night arise;
Your spring & your day are wasted in play
And your winter and night in disguise.

The SICK ROSE

O Rose thou art sick.
The invisible worm.
That flies in the night
In the howling storm:

Has found out thy bed
Of crimson joy:
And his dark secret love
Does thy life destroy.

The SICK ROSE

O Rose thou art sick.
The invisible worm,
That flies in the night
In the howling storm:

Has found out thy bed
Of crimson joy:
And his dark secret love
Does thy life destroy.

THE FLY.

Little Fly
Thy summers play,
My thoughtless hand
Has brush'd away.

Am not I
A fly like thee?
Or art not thou
A man like me?

For I dance
And drink & sing:
Till some blind hand
Shall brush my wing.

If thought is life
And strength & breath:
And the want
Of thought is death;

Then am I
A happy fly,
If I live,
Or if I die.

The Angel

I Dreamt a Dream, what can it mean.
And that I was a maiden Queen:
Guarded by an Angel mild:
Witless woe, was ne'er beguild!

And I wept both night and day
And he wip'd my tears away
And I wept both day and night
And hid from him my hearts delight

So he took his wings and fled:
Then the morn blush'd rosy red:
I dried my tears & armd my fears,
With ten thousand shields and spears.

Soon my Angel came again:
I was arm'd, he came in vain:
For the time of youth was fled
And grey hairs were on my head.

The Angel

I Dreamt a Dream! what can it mean?
And that I was a maiden Queen:
Guarded by an Angel mild:
Witless woe, was neer beguil'd!

And I wept both night and day
And he wip'd my tears away
And I wept both day and night
And hid from him my hearts delight

So he took his wings and fled:
Then the morn blush'd rosy red:
I dried my tears & armd my fears,
With ten thousand shields and spears.

Soon my Angel came again:
I was arm'd, he came in vain:
For the time of youth was fled
And grey hairs were on my head

The Tyger

Tyger Tyger, burning bright,
In the forests of the night;
What immortal hand or eye,
Could frame thy fearful symmetry?

In what distant deeps or skies,
Burnt the fire of thine eyes?
On what wings dare he aspire?
What the hand, dare sieze the fire?

And what shoulder, & what art,
Could twist the sinews of thy heart?
And when thy heart began to beat,
What dread hand? & what dread feet?

What the hammer? what the chain,
In what furnace was thy brain?
What the anvil? what dread grasp,
Dare its deadly terrors clasp?

When the stars threw down their spears
And water'd heaven with their tears:
Did he smile his work to see?
Did he who made the Lamb make thee?

Tyger Tyger burning bright,
In the forests of the night:
What immortal hand or eye,
Dare frame thy fearful symmetry?

The Tyger

Tyger Tyger, burning bright,
In the forests of the night!
What immortal hand or eye,
Could frame thy fearful symmetry?

In what distant deeps or skies
Burnt the fire of thine eyes!
On what wings dare he aspire!
What the hand, dare seize the fire?

And what shoulder, & what art,
Could twist the sinews of thy heart?
And when thy heart began to beat,
What dread hand? & what dread feet?

What the hammer? what the chain,
In what furnace was thy brain?
What the anvil? what dread grasp,
Dare its deadly terrors clasp!

When the stars threw down their spears
And water'd heaven with their tears:
Did he smile his work to see?
Did he who made the Lamb make thee?

Tyger Tyger burning bright,
In the forests of the night;
What immortal hand or eye,
Dare frame thy fearful symmetry?

My Pretty ROSE TREE

A flower was offerd to me:
Such a flower as May never bore.
But I said I've a Pretty Rose-tree.
And I passed the sweet flower oer.

Then I went to my Pretty Rose-tree:
To tend her by day and by night.
But my Rose turnd away with jealousy:
And her thorns were my only delight.

AH! SUN-FLOWER

Ah Sun-flower! weary of time.
Who countest the steps of the Sun:
Seeking after that sweet golden clime
Where the travellers journey is done.

Where the Youth pined away with desire,
And the pale Virgin shrouded in snow:
Arise from their graves and aspire,
Where my Sun-flower wishes to go.

THE LILLY

The modest Rose puts forth a thorn:
The humble Sheep. a threatning horn:
While the Lilly white, shall in Love delight,
Nor a thorn nor a threat stain her beauty bright

My Pretty ROSE TREE

A flower was offerd to me:
Such a flower as May never bore.
But I said I've a Pretty Rose-tree,
And I passed the sweet flower o'er.

Then I went to my Pretty Rose-tree:
To tend her by day and by night.
But my Rose turnd away with jealousy:
And her thorns were my only delight.

AH! SUN-FLOWER

Ah Sun-flower! weary of time,
Who countest the steps of the Sun:
Seeking after that sweet golden clime,
Where the travellers journey is done.

Where the Youth pined away with desire,
And the pale Virgin shrouded in snow:
Arise from their graves and aspire,
Where my Sun-flower wishes to go.

THE LILLY

The modest Rose puts forth a thorn:
The humble Sheep, a threatning horn:
While the Lilly white, shall in Love delight,
Nor a thorn nor a threat stain her beauty bright.

The GARDEN of LOVE

I went to the Garden of Love.
And saw what I never had seen:
A Chapel was built in the midst,
Where I used to play on the green.

And the gates of this Chapel were shut,
And Thou shalt not, writ over the door;
So I turn'd to the Garden of Love,
That so many sweet flowers bore,

And I saw it was filled with graves,
And tomb-stones where flowers should be:
And Priests in black gowns, were walking their rounds,
And binding with briars, my joys & desires.

The GARDEN of LOVE

I went to the Garden of Love.
And saw what I never had seen:
A Chapel was built in the midst,
Where I used to play on the green.

And the gates of this Chapel were shut,
And Thou shalt not. writ over the door:
So I turnd to the Garden of Love,
That so many sweet flowers bore.

And I saw it was filled with graves,
And tomb-stones where flowers should be:
And, Priests in black gowns, were walking their
    rounds,
And, binding with briars, my joys & desires.

The Little Vagabond

Dear Mother, dear Mother, the Church is cold.
But the Ale-house is healthy & pleasant & warm:
Besides I can tell where I am used well,
Such usage in heaven will never do well.

But if at the Church they would give us some Ale.
And a pleasant fire, our souls to regale;
We'd sing and we'd pray, all the live-long day;
Nor ever once wish from the Church to stray.

Then the Parson might preach & drink & sing.
And we'd be as happy as birds in the spring:
And modest dame Lurch, who is always at Church,
Would not have bandy children nor fasting nor birch.

And God like a father rejoicing to see,
His children as pleasant and happy as he:
Would have no more quarrel with the Devil or the Barrel
But kiss him & give him both drink and apparel.

The Little Vagabond

Dear Mother, dear Mother, the Church is cold.
But the Ale-house is healthy & pleasant & warm:
Besides I can tell where I am use'd well.
Such usage in heaven will never do well.

But if at the Church they would give us some Ale,
And a pleasant fire, our souls to regale:
We'd sing and we'd pray all the live-long day:
Nor ever once wish from the Church to stray.

Then the Parson might preach & drink & sing,
And we'd be as happy as birds in the spring:
And modest dame Lurch, who is always at Church,
Would not have bandy children nor fasting nor birch.

And God like a father rejoicing to see,
His children as pleasant and happy as he:
Would have no more quarrel with the Devil or the Barrel
But kiss him & give him both drink and apparel.

LONDON

I wander thro' each charter'd street,
Near where the charter'd Thames does flow
And mark in every face I meet
Marks of weakness, marks of woe.

In every cry of every Man,
In every Infants cry of fear,
In every voice; in every ban,
The mind-forg'd manacles I hear

How the Chimney-sweepers cry
Every blackning Church appalls,
And the hapless Soldiers sigh
Runs in blood down Palace walls

But most thro' midnight streets I hear
How the youthful Harlots curse
Blasts the new-born Infants tear
And blights with plagues the Marriage hearse

LONDON

I wander thro' each charter'd street,
Near where the charter'd Thames does flow
And mark in every face I meet
Marks of weakness, marks of woe.

In every cry of every Man,
In every Infants cry of fear,
In every voice: in every ban,
The mind-forg'd manacles I hear

How the Chimney-sweepers cry
Every blackning Church appalls,
And the hapless Soldiers sigh,
Runs in blood down Palace walls

But most thro' midnight streets I hear
How the youthful Harlots curse
Blasts the new-born Infants tear
And blights with plagues the Marriage hearse

The Human Abstract.

Pity would be no more,
If we did not make somebody Poor;
And Mercy no more could be,
If all were as happy as we;

And mutual fear brings peace;
Till the selfish loves increase.
Then Cruelty knits a snare,
And spreads his baits with care.

He sits down with holy fears,
And waters the ground with tears:
Then Humility takes its root
Underneath his foot.

Soon spreads the dismal shade
Of Mystery over his head;
And the Catterpiller and Fly,
Feed on the Mystery.

And it bears the fruit of Deceit,
Ruddy and sweet to eat;
And the Raven his nest has made
In its thickest shade.

The Gods of the earth and sea,
Sought thro' Nature to find this Tree;
But their search was all in vain:
There grows one in the Human Brain

The Human Abstract.

Pity would be no more,
If we did not make somebody Poor:
And Mercy no more could be,
If all were as happy as we:

And mutual fear brings peace:
Till the selfish loves increase.
Then Cruelty knits a snare,
And spreads his baits with care.

He sits down with holy fears,
And waters the ground with tears:
Then Humility takes its root
Underneath his foot.

Soon spreads the dismal shade
Of Mystery over his head;
And the Catterpiller and Fly,
Feed on the Mystery.

And it bears the fruit of Deceit,
Ruddy and sweet to eat:
And the Raven his nest has made
In its thickest shade.

The Gods of the earth and sea,
Sought thro' Nature to find this Tree
But their search was all in vain;
There grows one in the Human Brain

INFANT SORROW

My mother groand! my father wept.
Into the dangerous world I leapt:
Helpless, naked, piping loud:
Like a fiend hid in a cloud.

Struggling in my fathers hands:
Striving against my swadling bands:
Bound and weary I thought best
To sulk upon my mothers breast.

INFANT SORROW

My mother groand! my father wept.
Into the dangerous world I leapt:
Helpless naked, piping loud;
Like a fiend hid in a cloud.

Struggling in my fathers hands:
Striving against my swadling bands
Bound and weary I thought best
To sulk upon my mothers breast.

A POISON TREE.

I was angry with my friend:
I told my wrath, my wrath did end.
I was angry with my foe:
I told it not, my wrath did grow.

And I waterd it in fears,
Night & morning with my tears:
And I sunned it with smiles,
And with soft deceitful wiles.

And it grew both day and night.
Till it bore an apple bright.
And my foe beheld it shine,
And he knew that it was mine.

And into my garden stole,
When the night had veild the pole;
In the morning glad I see;
My foe outstretchd beneath the tree.

A POISON TREE.

I was angry with my friend:
I told my wrath, my wrath did end.
I was angry with my foe:
I told it not, my wrath did grow.

And I waterd it in fears,
Night & morning with my tears:
And I sunned it with smiles,
And with soft deceitful wiles.

And it grew both day and night,
Till it bore an apple bright.
And my foe beheld it shine,
And he knew that it was mine.

And into my garden stole,
When the night had veild the pole;
In the morning glad I see,
My foe outstretchd beneath the tree.

A Little BOY Lost

Nought loves another as itself
Nor venerates another so,
Nor is it possible to Thought
A greater than itself to know:

And Father, how can I love you,
Or any of my brothers more?
I love you like the little bird
That picks up crumbs around the door.

The Priest sat by and heard the child,
In trembling zeal he siez'd his hair:
He led him by his little coat:
And all admir'd the Priestly care.

And standing on the altar high,
Lo what a fiend is here! said he:
One who sets reason up for judge
Of our most holy Mystery.

The weeping child could not be heard,
The weeping parents wept in vain:
They strip'd him to his little shirt,
And bound him in an iron chain.

And burn'd him in a holy place,
Where many had been burn'd before:
The weeping parents wept in vain.
Are such things done on Albions shore.

A Little BOY Lost

Nought loves another as itself,
Nor venerates another so,
Nor is it possible to thought
A greater than itself to know:

And Father, how can I love you,
Or any of my brothers more?
I love you like the little bird
That picks up crumbs around the door.

The Priest sat by and heard the child,
In trembling zeal he siez'd his hair:
He led him by his little coat:
And all admir'd the Priestly care.

And standing on the altar high,
Lo what a fiend is here! said he:
One who sets reason up for judge
Of our most holy Mystery.

The weeping child could not be heard,
The weeping parents wept in vain:
They strip'd him to his little shirt,
And bound him in an iron chain

And burn'd him in a holy place
Where many had been burn'd before:
The weeping parents wept in vain.
Are such things done on Albions shore

A Little GIRL Lost

Children of the future Age,
Reading this indignant page;
Know that in a former time
Love! sweet Love! was thought a crime

In the Age of Gold,
Free from winters cold:
Youth and maiden bright,
To the holy light,
Naked in the sunny beams delight.

Once a youthful pair
Filld with sweetest care;
Met in garden bright,
Where the holy light,
Had just removd the curtains of the night

There in rising day,
On the grass they play:
Parents were afar;
Strangers came not near;
And the maiden soon forgot her fear.

Tired with kisses sweet
They agree to meet,
When the silent sleep
Waves oer heavens deep;
And the weary tired wanderers weep.

To her father white
Came the maiden bright:
But his loving look,
Like the holy book,
All her tender limbs with terror shook.

Ona! pale and weak!
To thy father speak:
O the trembling fear!
O the dismal care!
That shakes the blossoms of my hoary hair

A Little GIRL Lost

Children of the future Age,
Reading this indignant page;
Know that in a former time,
Love! sweet Love! was thought a crime.

In the Age of Gold,
Free from winters cold:
Youth and maiden bright,
To the holy light,
Naked in the sunny beams
        delight.

Once a youthful pair
Fill'd with softest care:
Met in garden bright,
Where the holy light,
Had just removd the curtains
        of the night.

There in rising day,
On the grass they play:
Parents were afar:
Strangers came not near:
And the maiden soon forgot
        her fear.

Tired with kisses sweet
They agree to meet,
When the silent sleep
Waves o'er heavens deep;
And the weary tired wanderers
        weep.

To her father white
Came the maiden bright:
But his loving look,
Like the holy book,
All her tender limbs with terror
        shook.

Ona! pale and weak!
To thy father speak:
O the trembling fear!
O the dismal care!
That shakes the blossoms of my
        hoary hair

To Tirzah

Whate'er is Born of Mortal Birth,
Must be consumed with the Earth
To rise from Generation free:
Then what have I to do with thee?

The Sexes sprung from Shame & Pride
Blowd in the morn; in evening died
But Mercy changd Death into Sleep;
The Sexes rose to work & weep.

Thou Mother of my Mortal part,
With cruelty didst mould my Heart.
And with false self-decieving tears,
Didst bind my Nostrils Eyes & Ears.

Didst close my Tongue in senseless clay
And me to Mortal Life betray:
The Death of Jesus set me free.
Then what have I to do with thee?

It is Raised
a Spiritual Body.

To Tirzah

Whate'er is Born of Mortal Birth
Must be consumed with the Earth
To rise from Generation free:
Then what have I to do with thee?

The Sexes sprung from Shame & Pride
Blow'd in the morn; in evening died
But Mercy changd Death into Sleep;
The Sexes rose to work & weep.

Thou Mother of my Mortal part
With cruelty didst mould my Heart
And with false self-deceiving tears
Didst bind my Nostrils Eyes & Ears

Didst close my Tongue in senseless clay
And me to Mortal Life betray
The Death of Jesus set me free
Then what have I to do with thee?

It is Raised a Spiritual Body

The School Boy

I love to rise in a summer morn,
When the birds sing on every tree;
The distant huntsman winds his horn,
And the sky-lark sings with me.
O; what sweet company.

But to go to school in a summer morn,
O; it drives all joy away;
Under a cruel eye outworn
The little ones spend the day,
In sighing and dismay.

Ah; then at times I drooping sit,
And spend many an anxious hour,
Nor in my book can I take delight,
Nor sit in learnings bower,
Worn thro' with the dreary shower.

How can the bird that is born for joy,
Sit in a cage and sing.
How can a child when fears annoy,
But droop his tender wing.
And forget his youthful spring.

O; father & mother, if buds are nipd,
And blossoms blown away,
And if the tender plants are strip'd
Of their joy in the springing day,
By sorrow and cares dismay.

How shall the summer arise in joy,
Or the summer fruits appear.
Or how shall we gather what griefs destroy
Or bless the mellowing year,
When the blasts of winter appear.

The School-Boy

I love to rise in a summer morn,
When the birds sing on every tree;
The distant huntsman winds his horn,
And the sky-lark sings with me.
O! what sweet company.

But to go to school in a summer morn,
O! it drives all joy away;
Under a cruel eye outworn,
The little ones spend the day,
In sighing and dismay.

Ah! then at times I drooping sit,
And spend many an anxious hour,
Nor in my book can I take delight,
Nor sit in learnings bower,
Worn thro' with the dreary shower.

How can the bird that is born for joy,
Sit in a cage and sing.
How can a child when fears annoy,
But droop his tender wing,
And forget his youthful spring.

O! father & mother, if buds are nip'd,
And blossoms blown away,
And if the tender plants are strip'd
Of their joy in the springing day,
By sorrow and cares dismay,

How shall the summer arise in joy
Or the summer fruits appear.
Or how shall we gather what griefs destroy
Or bless the mellowing year,
When the blasts of winter appear.

The Voice of the Ancient Bard.

Youth of delight come hither,
And see the opening morn,
Image of truth new born.
Doubt is fled & clouds of reason,
Dark disputes & artful teazing.
Folly is an endless maze.
Tangled roots perplex her ways,
How many have fallen there!
They stumble all night over bones of the dead:
And feel they know not what but care:
And wish to lead others when they should be led

It would seem from its title that this poem was intended to be the contrary poem to 'The Divine Image' of *Innocence*. It can be interpreted as providing the disillusioning discovery that human nature in its most evil moments can exhibit the very opposite of the attributes described in *Innocence*: It is possible that the poem was designed as a late addition or alternative theme for *Experience*, written perhaps during a violent revulsion of feeling produced by the war with France.

The extreme violence of Blake's feelings is exhibited in the design. It shews Los, the poet and craftsman, forging the Sun, symbol of imagination, into the words of his poem with furious blows of his creative sledge-hammer on the anvil. Afterwards Blake saw that his verses were even more savage than he had intended, and so he abandoned them, though he did not destroy the plate. It is known only as an uncoloured print made a few years after Blake's death.

A DIVINE IMAGE

Cruelty has a Human Heart
And Jealousy a Human Face
Terror, the Human Form Divine
And Secrecy, the Human Dress

The Human Dress, is forged Iron
The Human Form, a fiery Forge.
The Human Face, a Furnace seal'd
The Human Heart, its hungry Gorge.

A DIVINE IMAGE

Cruelty has a Human Heart
And Jealousy a Human Face
Terror. the Human Form Divine
And Secrecy. the Human Dress

The Human Dress. is forged Iron
The Human Form. a fiery Forge
The Human Face. a Furnace seal'd
The Human Heart. its hungry Gorge.

The Commentary

SONGS Of INNOCENCE
and Of EXPERIENCE
Shewing the Two Contrary States of the Human Soul

Below the title are the figures of fallen Man represented as
Adam and Eve. They are girdled with leaves, shewing that they
are in a state of Experience. Tongues of flame playing over them
indicate their expulsion from Eden, while the bird of Innocence
flying overhead has escaped the flames.

Pl. 2   Frontispiece to *Songs of Innocence*

The scene is a literal illustration of the first poem, entitled
'Introduction'. The poet is represented as a shepherd with a pipe
in his hands looking up at the vision of a child above his head.
His sheep are behind him; on either side and in the background
are trees, a symbol not mentioned in the poem. Trees of different
kinds signified for Blake varying aspects of life on earth; their
leaves are in the sky, but their roots are firmly buried in the
ground. The twining trunks of the tree on the poet's left symbo-
lize earthly love.

Pl. 3   Title-page

SONGS of Innocence
1789
The Author & Printer W Blake

In the decoration two children stand at their mother's knee
reading a book. Over them arches a broken apple tree bearing a

few fruits, with a vine twisting round its trunk—the fruitful symbol of Christianity embracing the tree of sinful life. The letters of the first word are bursting into vegetable growths; among them are small figures and birds, symbols of joy. Leaning against the *I* of *Innocence*, in this copy indistinctly drawn, is a man in a wide hat, such as Blake wore, playing on a pipe (see below). The date 1789, under the right branch of the tree, is also indistinct in this copy.

An enlarged detail from the electrotype
of Blake's original plate.

Pl. 4   INTRODUCTION

In this preliminary poem Blake sets the scene for his *Songs*, imagining himself, the poet, as a shepherd wandering in an Arcadian valley and piping to his sheep. With the vision of the child on a cloud he sees himself being directed by the innocent spirit of poetry, and is bidden to pipe a song about a lamb, itself the symbol of innocence. Both child and lamb are symbols, too, of religion in the person of Jesus. The poet is then told to drop his pipe and sing his songs, and finally to write them in a book, using the materials ready to his hand—coloured water with a reed as pen. The last line points to children as his audience, though it is the innocent in heart, whether child or adult, that he means.

The decorations on either side of the text are derived from a mediæval manuscript illustrating the Tree of Jesse, though the tiny figures within each loop are indistinctly drawn.

Pl. 5   THE SHEPHERD

The second poem is a simple one and needs little comment. The shepherd has now put down his pipe and holds a crook instead, the sign of his calling. The two stanzas express the relationship of the ewes and their lambs with their guardian, the shepherd. All is Arcadian peace and trustfulness. A bird of paradise soars into the sky; on the shepherd's left is a tree with a flowering plant twining up its trunk.

Pls. 6 and 7   THE ECCHOING GREEN

The theme of this poem was anticipated in an earlier 'Song' printed among the *Poetical Sketches* in 1783:

> I love the laughing vale
> I love the ecchoing hill
>
> .   .   .
>
> I love the oaken seat
> Beneath the oaken tree
> Where all the villagers meet
> And laugh our sports to see.

In 'The Ecchoing Green' the first stanza assembles all the joyful symbols of the Spring in nature and young humanity. In the second stanza the elder folk, identified as Old John and three motherly women, sit on a bench surrounding an oak tree, while youths and children sport around them. The third stanza is illustrated in the second plate, where Old John is seen leading the tired children home to their rest at sunset.

The oak on the village green is the symbol of strength and security. Later it became connected in Blake's mind with the cruel religion of the Druids, but here it is the guardian of young and old.

The delicately coiling vines in the lower part of the first plate have on the second plate turned into a sturdier growth, perhaps a Tree of Life, with heavy bunches of grapes hanging from its branches. The two boys of the first plate with bat and hoop have become youths plucking the ripe grapes, one of them handing a bunch down to a girl below. They are on the road to Experience, passing from the age of Innocence to that of sexual awareness. The boys on the ground with kite and bat are still in a state of childish innocence.

Pl. 8   THE LAMB

Rightly regarded as one of Blake's most triumphantly successful poems, this is also one of his most transparent. The lamb and the child, both symbols of innocence and of religion, converse together, the child properly supplying both question and answer. They are illustrated together in the design, with a cottage to one side and the oak of security in the background. On either side are delicate saplings arching over the scene without any overtones of Experience.

Pls. 9 and 10   THE LITTLE BLACK BOY

The little black boy sitting at his mother's knee seems in the first stanza to deplore the blackness of his face, since it hides the purity of his soul, whereas the English child is white both inside and out. His mother, looking towards the rising sun, explains how God gives warmth and comfort to all living things by the light of the sun. The boy's black face is but a temporary cloud, a protection, even, from the extreme heat and light of the Sun God. In the penultimate stanza the boy picks up this theme and explains to the English child that they are really both the same, each being clouded by his body until he reaches a spiritual state of joy 'round the tent of God'. He even regards himself as the stronger of the two, acting as guardian and stroking the silver hair of the other until they love one another as equals. In the second illustration the two boys stand before God personified as Christ, the Good Shepherd, with his crook. He sits beside a stream with a willowy tree arching over his haloed head, the water and the vegetation indicating that heaven may be found upon earth.

The poem probably was to some extent inspired by contemporary indignation against slavery and the supposed inferiority of black races, but it also teaches that the creation of the world was an act of divine mercy, by which man might become accustomed to endure the heat of divine love.

Pl. 11   THE BLOSSOM

This lovely little poem, at first sight seeming to have but slight meaning, is in truth a poetical expression of the consummation of love by the act of generation. The sparrow 'swift as arrow' is a phallic symbol seeking satisfaction in the blossom of the maiden's bosom. The robin sobs perhaps with the happiness of experience. The cryptic symbolism carries the meaning of the poem with the utmost delicacy, and it is equalled by the beauty of the design. This illustrates the organ of generation both flaccid and erect, with the generative principle breaking from its crest in the form of tiny winged and happy figures. One has found its goal in the maiden's bosom; she sits contentedly among the flying joys, distinguished by her green dress and large angel's wings, since she, with her prospective motherhood, is an ideal figure to the male during the act of generation.

The poem 'Infant Joy' is closely related to 'The Blossom', though separated from it in this copy of the *Songs* by several other poems.

Pl. 12   THE CHIMNEY SWEEPER

This poem in narrative form begins with a line of prose and ends with a seemingly commonplace moral. It is evidently related to the earlier poem, 'The Little Black Boy', being again inspired by indignation—this time against the shameful use of small boys for sweeping chimneys, the white boy being blackened by the soot of human cruelty. It has been suggested that the name Tom Dacre was formed by transposition of the letters in Tom Dark. The 'weep, weep' of his cry in the street is both a Cockney version of the sweep's profession and a realization of his misery. Many years after its composition Charles Lamb chose this poem as a contribution to James Montgomery's *Chimney Sweeper's Friend and Climbing Boy's Album*, 1824, a book of propaganda against social injustice. In Blake's poem the Angel of Tom's dream unlocks the coffin of his unhappy circumstances and sets his spirit free to float on clouds of the imaginative life. It is perhaps living this life that is the 'duty' of the last line.

The decoration at the bottom of the plate shews the Angel unlocking the coffin and the boys rejoicing in their freedom.

Pl. 13   THE LITTLE BOY LOST

In this poem and the next the child represents the human spirit seeking the conventional 'God', or Father, promised to our childish minds, but proving to be non-existent as we flounder in the mire of the material world. The Father is represented in the illustration by a bright Will-o'-the-Wisp misleading the child among the menacing trees of life on earth. The text is surrounded by angelic figures and stars, perhaps representing salvation by the life of the imagination if we can see it.

Pl. 14   THE LITTLE BOY FOUND

This continuation of the preceding verses shews the child rescued by a person in the image of God leading him out of the forest to his sorrowing mother. She is shewn on the right of the text as a figure with arms stretched out ready to receive him. Both the child and his mother are sanctified by possessing halos; this can only mean that man has been restored to the life of the imagination and thereby saved.

The rescuer's form is ostensibly female, so appearing to be in disagreement with the poem. Probably it is one of Blake's not infrequent androgynous figures, having both mother and father attributes.

Pl. 15   LAUGHING SONG

The 'Laughing Song' is simplicity itself, and seems to mean exactly what it says. It is, moreover, literally a song for singing. Blake was said by those who knew him sometimes to sing his poems to tunes of his own composing, and here 'the sweet chorus of Ha, Ha, He' calls for a simple merry tune. The youth standing in the centre of the party seen in the illustration, with his hat and wine-cup held in his hands, is clearly the leader of the chorus.

Pls. 16 and 17   A CRADLE SONG

Blake's 'Cradle Song' conforms in its simplicity to the general pattern of all lullabies and calls for little comment.

The dreamy tangles of the falling vegetation decorating the margins of the first plate suggest the feeling of the first line:

Sweet dreams form a shade.

A few indeterminate figures can be made out among the tendrils; one of these near the top on the right, a soft female form hovering with arms stretched out in benison, seems to be suggested by the third and fourth lines of the second verse:

Sweet sleep Angel mild,
Hover o'er my happy child.

The illustration on the second plate is uncompromising in the hard outlines of the mother's clumsy chair and the child's wicker cot. Yet a subtle touch is in accord with the transference in the last two verses where the child's image is replaced by that of the infant Jesus—it is surely not by chance that the child's pillow is so arranged as to form a conspicuous halo around its head.

Pl. 18   THE DIVINE IMAGE

In this poem Blake has expressed one of his most deeply felt themes—the identification of man with God. Many passages can be found throughout his writings illustrating his fundamental belief in the divinity of human nature. God had revealed Himself as a man in the person of Christ, and so a great and good man is to be reverenced as if he were God:

> Human Nature is the image of God (Annotations to Lavater's *Aphorisms*, c.1788). The worship of God is: Honouring his gift in other men . . . those who envy or calumniate great men hate God; for there is no other God (*Marriage of Heaven and Hell*, Pl. 22, c.1790). God is Man & exists in us & we in him (Annotations to Berkeley's *Siris*, c.1820)

and so on in many variations. The poem with its steady repetitive beat hammers in the theme that Mercy, Pity, Peace and Love are attributes both human and divine.

Accordingly the decoration is a symbol of human life—a strange flame-like growth, half vegetable and half fire, twined with flowering plants. At its origin below, a Christ-like figure raises man and woman from the earth. At the top small human forms 'pray in their distress', while behind them an angel commits them to the care of Mercy, Pity, Peace and Love, personified as a woman in a green dress.

In 'Holy Thursday' Blake described an annual event in St. Paul's Cathedral, which he had no doubt witnessed. The poem sounds sentimental, but more probably it was ironic. The 'event' was the marching of some six thousand of the poorest children from the charity schools of London into St. Paul's guided by their Beadles for a compulsory exhibition of their piety and gratitude to their patrons. Blake's true feelings about this were expressed in the corresponding poem in *Songs of Experience*, where the social injustice of poverty and charity is roundly condemned. Only in the last line does more genuine feeling become apparent. Even though the existence of so much poverty was wrong, at least pity was allowable.

The irony (if that is right) is driven home by the regimented and uniformed processions of children depicted at the top and bottom of the plate.

Pls. 20 and 21   NIGHT

The theme of this poem, celebrating the gentle delights of a summer's night, was anticipated in a shorter lyric, 'To the Evening Star', printed in *Poetical Sketches*. In 'Night', where the idea has perhaps become an allegory of death, it is elaborated and given a metrical form of great beauty. In previous poems the cruelty of man was noticed; in this poem the cruelty of Nature is introduced, with promise of its disappearance in another world.

In the decorations, the lion is seen on the right of the first plate, crouching in his den beneath a tree, but a winged figure is poised over him and others have alighted on the upper branches of the tree. Several more extend up the left-hand margin towards the moon. The evening star is shining on the right in some copies of the book, though not in this one. In the second plate five angels with conspicuous halos are walking on the grass ready to receive the 'mild spirits'. Three more are indistinctly seen in the branches of the tree in the left margin. The whole plate has the deep blue colouring of night, with stars shewing through the branches of the tree on the right.

Pls. 22 and 23   SPRING

The exquisite texture of this poem defies comment. Its reckless rhymes and half-rhymes run on to end in the refrain of each stanza. Almost without structure, yet the lines express precisely the joyful feeling of spring-time.

The decorative spirals on each plate harbouring small winged figures, with the recurrent conjunction of child and lamb, match perfectly with the simple theme.

Pl. 24   NURSE'S SONG

The four stanzas of this poem express with perfect simplicity the happy irresponsibility of childhood. As one critic has said—'few besides Blake could have written such a successful poem on the delight of being allowed to play a little longer until dusk'.

The decoration shows the nurse watching the children dancing merrily in a circle. The weeping willow in the right-hand margin is perhaps a reminder that not all life is fun and games.

Pl. 25   INFANT JOY

The apparent simplicity of this delicate poem and the obvious beauty of the illustration have deceived some critics into taking it at its face value. It has already been mentioned as related to another poem, 'The Blossom', regarded as an expression of the consummation of love. 'Infant Joy', seemingly so innocent, may be understood to shew the consequences of 'The Blossom'—the conception of a new life. S. T. Coleridge criticized the poem for its inaccuracy. An infant two days old, he said, cannot smile. But neither can it speak, as it does in the first stanza, so that poetic licence must be given full rein. The illustration reveals the true nature of the verses. The unidentifiable plant has on one stem an unopened bud—an unimpregnated womb. The open flower above is the impregnated womb with the newly conceived infant lying on its mother's lap. Before them stands a winged messenger—the scene is an 'annunciation'; the second stanza may be the words of the mother or of the messenger, or both.

In a very early copy of the *Songs of Innocence*, the sepals of the flower have been painted the same colour as the petals. This error has been attributed to Mrs. Blake, though Blake himself was not always an accurate naturalist. In this copy the proper colours give greater beauty to the design as a whole.

Pl. 26   A DREAM

In this poem Blake has composed a simple fable which may perhaps be understood as a statement of the human predicament in terms of the lowest animal creation. The narrator, himself secure and 'Angel-guarded', dreams of an ant lost in the grass and anxious for her children. He is about to bewail her fate with tears when the 'watchman of the night' appears in the shape of a glow-worm and undertakes, with the help of the beetle, to guide her home. Thus the human spirit lost in the 'forests of the night' is portrayed by an allegory of the sorrows besetting the most insignificant of God's creatures. But even the ant is not uncared for and is led to safety by the glow-worm's light, the humble messenger of divine compassion.

The simple decoration includes only one figure—the 'watchman of the night', in the lower right-hand corner.

Pl. 27   ON ANOTHERS SORROW

In 'A Dream' Blake's narrator was grieving for the sorrows of the ant. The same pity for 'another's woe' is expressed at greater length in the nine stanzas of the present poem, human troubles being illustrated by those of small creatures—infants and small birds. Divine compassion and help is promised by the coming of Christ, first as an infant and then as a man of sorrows, who will assuage our sorrows by his own.

The decoration is again simple. On the right is a leafy tree with a vine coiling up its stem; a bird of paradise takes wing from its branches. On the left are vague human figures climbing up to safety.

Pl. 28   Frontispiece to *Songs of Experience*

This design is contrasted with the frontispiece to *Songs of Innocence* by the different aspect of the youth portrayed. In the first he was the Shepherd in a state of Innocence still in charge of his sheep. In the second he is stepping with his right foot forward to leave his flock behind and advance into the state of Experience. The visionary child of the first picture has now been transformed into a winged cherub invested (in this copy of the book) with a halo and seated on the young man's head. The youth secures the boy's balance by holding his hands with his own. The symbol is not easy to understand, though it seems possible that it originated from *Ezekiel* xxviii.14, where the Prophet likens the King of Tyre to the cherubim seated on the Ark of the Covenant, saying: 'Thou art the anointed cherub that covereth', but adding that the King had sinned because of his great riches. Thus 'the Covering Cherub' came to represent the corruption following Experience. The phrase was often used by Blake in his longer epics to mean the Selfhood, 'that self-seeking, which is the root of all Christian errors' (Damon).

The tree trunk on the youth's left has ivy climbing up it, the unpleasant shapes of the leaves indicating the troubles inherent in Experience.

Pl. 29   Title-page

SONGS of EXPERIENCE

1794

The Author & Printer W Blake

The design on this title-page is conspicuously hard, with the word EXPERIENCE set like a bar across the page. This is accentuated by the formality of the architectural background to the figures below—two young people, arrived at the age of Experience, mourning beside the bodies of the parents whose guidance they have lost. It has been conjectured (Damon) that the arrangement of these figures is intended to suggest a Cross. Between the words SONGS and EXPERIENCE are a naked man and a clothed maiden flying towards one another with arms outstretched in anticipation of the pleasures of love, but between them are ivy leaves, suggesting by their spiky shapes the pains of sex-love and experience.

Pl. 30   INTRODUCTION

In his 'Introduction' to the state of Experience Blake sees himself as the Ancient Bard, the Prophet, who heard Jehovah speaking to Adam in the Garden; he calls the Fallen Man to regain control of the world, lost when he adopted Reason (the 'starry pole') in place of Imagination. Earth is the symbol of the Fallen Man, who is summoned to awake from materialism and to turn again to the free life of the imagination. The 'starry floor' of Reason and the 'wat'ry shore' of the Sea of Time and Space (the edge of materialism) are there only till the break of day if Earth would consent to leave 'the slumberous mass'.

The decoration shews Earth as a female figure reclining on a couch borne on a cloud among a night of stars. In this copy her head is surrounded by a golden circle through which she looks at the Universe.

Pl. 31   EARTH'S ANSWER

In the answer to the Bard's call in the 'Introduction' Earth
replies that she is a prisoner of Reason and of the jealous creator
of the material world (afterwards named Urizen by Blake). Free
love is demanded as typifying the life of freedom lost by the fall of
man in Eden.

The decorations are for the most part simple vegetation of the
material world. The snake below, perhaps the Serpent of the
Garden of Eden, symbolizes for Blake the priesthood with their
denial of freedom for natural energies.

Pl. 32   THE CLOD & THE PEBBLE

In this poem the Clod of Clay, soft and pliable compared with the
hard Pebble, sings the song of unselfish love and so of Innocence,
thus building a Heaven to the despair of the Hell of selfishness.
The Pebble, lying immobile in the waters of materialism,
symbolizes the contrary state of Experience, singing the song of
selfish love and building a Hell in spite of Heaven. A great deal
more can be read into the dialectics of the poem with its obvious
reference to the book, *The Marriage of Heaven and Hell*, written
earlier than *Songs of Experience*. The Clod of Clay had also
appeared in *The Book of Thel*, where it is the lowliest thing in
the created world.

The upper illustration shews the sheep of Innocence (though
perhaps not now so innocent, since they consist of a ram, two
ewes and a lamb) side by side with the heavy bull and cow of
Experience drinking the water of materialism. In the lower
illustration a duck floats on the water, with frogs and a worm,
each in turn preying on the other.

Pl. 33   HOLY THURSDAY

It was suggested that 'Holy Thursday' in *Songs of Innocence* was perhaps a satire on the annual parade of charity children in St. Paul's Cathedral. In this corresponding poem of *Experience* Blake makes a more direct and powerful attack on the shameful presence of so much poverty 'in a rich and fruitful land'. The spiritual state of such a country is eternal winter contrasted with the sunshine enjoyed by a more just society.

The upper illustration shews a mother standing beneath a leafless tree growing on 'the wat'ry shore' of the 'Introduction'; she gazes at the lifeless body of her infant. In the right-hand margin are other scenes of poverty and death.

Pls. 34, 35 and 36   THE LITTLE GIRL LOST
                          THE LITTLE GIRL FOUND

The two poems of 'The Little Girl Lost' and 'Found', together forming a long ballad of Life and Death, were originally composed by Blake for the *Songs of Innocence*. The first two stanzas shew that the idea of himself as the Prophetic Bard was already in his mind. He predicts that Earth, or mankind, will one day regard death as a release into a pleasant garden in Christ's presence. The human soul is personified as a child named Lyca, living in the sleeping world of Experience. She is found in her sleep by the Lion, here meaning the Angel of Death, who removes her covering of flesh and, with the other animals (none of which, according to a mediæval belief, could harm a virgin), takes her to his cave. Meanwhile Lyca's parents, wandering through the troubles of this life in search of her, themselves meet the Lion, but the Angel of Death is transformed into 'A Spirit arm'd in gold', who leads them to their still sleeping child. They then dwell together in the eternal 'garden mild' of the first stanza.

The decoration on the first plate seems at first to have no relation to the poem until it is noticed that the girl, with her lover, is pointing up to the first prophetic stanzas, whence a bird takes flight. The symbolic serpent turns away on the other side, frustrated by the truth of the Bard's prophecy. In the second plate Lyca is seen about to sleep beneath one of the trees of earthly life. Below, a beast of prey seems to scent his victim. On the third plate children are playing in paradise with the harmless lions beside the twining trees of love. A figure resembling Earth of the 'Introduction' lies unconcernedly beside them.

Pl. 37   THE CHIMNEY SWEEPER

In the corresponding poem in *Songs of Innocence* the little chimney sweep appeared wholly miserable until released by the Angel. In *Experience* the boy is still sometimes happy, but tells of his exploitation by his parents, who imagine they are not wronging him because his spirit is not wholly subdued. The 'holy' parents are in church since the Church condoned the society able to inflict such cruelty on the innocent child.

The illustration is literal, shewing the boy with his bag of soot in the snow.

Pl. 38   NURSES SONG

This 'song' is a parody of the corresponding poem in *Songs of Innocence*. The difference is emphasized by the form of the title— 'NURSES Song' instead of 'Nurse's Song'. In this poem the words are spoken only by the nurse. The children, with their 'whisp'rings in the dale', are no longer real children, but are adolescents aware of sex. The nurse recalls with regret how she wasted her spring-time without real gratification, and tells the 'children' that their winter and night will be spoiled by repression and hypocrisy. Her face turns 'green and pale' because that is traditionally the colour of the sex-starved spinster, sick with longings for experiences which will never be hers.

In the illustration an adolescent boy is allowing his hair to be combed by the nurse; we are to assume his repressed resentment of the woman's power over him and his secret resolution to rebel.

His more docile sister sits quietly behind him. The evil of female domination, so destructive of the male personality, already explicit in this poem, was often in Blake's mind, as we know from passages in other writings. The cottage door from which the boy has come is conspicuously wreathed with vines, symbol of the pleasures he will find in life.

Pl. 39   THE SICK ROSE

This poem is usually interpreted as an image of the troubles of earthly love. The symbolism of a red rose for corporeal love and of the worm (or the flesh) for the source of the sickness is plain. In the illustration a worm (banded like an earthworm in some copies) is entering the heart of the rose and simultaneously the spirit of joy is extruded. The 'howling storm' in which the worm comes is a symbol of materialism. The bush from which the rose has bent down to the ground presents several other details. On the left is a 'catterpiller' (always spelt thus by Blake) feeding on a leaf, the creature being for him, as for the Bible and the Elizabethan poets, the symbol of the 'pillager' or despoiler. Elsewhere Blake denoted the 'catterpiller' as the chief enemy of the rose, equating it with the priesthood, who lay their curses on the fairest joys. Further down the stems are two figures in attitudes of despair. The menacing thorns scattered along the whole length of the stems emphasize the pains of love on earth.

Pl. 40   THE FLY

In the short, flickering lines of this poem Blake imitates the flight of an insect darting to and fro. He likens himself to the insect, which chance might destroy at any moment. This is not to say that he, as a man, is unimportant, but that the fly, like any other living creature, has significance, so that Blake himself is like a happy fly, dead or alive.

The design illustrates the cheerful inconsequence of man's life as shewn by children at play, the shuttlecock perhaps being meant to resemble an insect on the wing. Over the group the dead tree of materialism extends its branches.

Pl. 41   THE ANGEL

The poet here imagines himself to be a woman dreaming of love. As a child she had been petted and Angel-guarded. Now she simulates grief to attract pitying attention, and hides her love, so that the Angel flies away. Then her mood changes, and when the Angel returns he finds her hardened by age. Love has come too late and is rejected.

This highly psychological poem is illustrated by a rather ordinary scene of the self-constituted maiden-Queen exacting pity from a winged Cupid for her simulated grief.

Pl. 42   THE TYGER

In fashioning his poem, 'The Tyger', Blake used inspired care in order to attain the effect he wanted to create. His three versions, two in manuscript and one on the etched plate, shew the stages through which his mind worked in achieving one of the finest and most profound poems in the English language. To some readers the result seems to be 'pure poetry', because its superb poetical form conveys no communicable meaning. For others the message must be made clear by picking the symbolism apart until its components appear to form a plain sequence. That this is in fact impossible becomes evident from the various attempts to do so, no one commentator ever agreeing with any other. It seems better, therefore, to let the poem speak for itself, the hammer strokes of the craftsman conveying to each mind some part of his meaning. The poem is deliberately composed of a series of questions, none of which is answered. It contains the riddle of the universe, how to reconcile good with evil. Careful dissection will only spoil its impact as poetry.

Even the illustration of a tiger, supposedly 'the Tyger of Wrath', standing beneath a tree is not as clear as it seems at first. In some copies of the book the animal is a ferocious carnivore painted in lurid colours. In others it appears to smile as if it were a tame cat. Perhaps Blake did not intend to dispel the mystery of his poem by painting an animal of consistent or obvious character.

Pl. 43

MY PRETTY ROSE TREE

AH! SUN-FLOWER

THE LILLY

This trilogy of short lyrics resembles musical variations on a theme—different aspects of love. Flowers are time-honoured symbols of love, and the first lyric repeats the symbol of 'The Sick Rose'. The situation is one that might have occurred between Blake and his wife or any other married couple. Extra-marital love is offered to the man. He rejects this by asserting his marital faithfulness, but on returning to his wife is met only with the thorns of reproaches and complaints.

In the second lyric the sun-flower, with its face always turned towards the sun while its roots are planted firmly in the ground, is a natural symbol of man's aspirations. In this context, the youth with his human desires and the maiden shrouded in frigid modesty both turn towards the setting sun where life ends, in the hope that their instincts may find satisfaction in the next world.

In the third lyric the white 'Lilly', symbol of innocent and honest love, is contrasted with the hypocrisy of the rose with its mock-modesty and the sheep with its simulated courage.

The only decoration is the generally applicable scene of a love-sick youth crouching at the feet of an apparently indifferent maiden.

Pl. 44   THE GARDEN OF LOVE

Flowers being the symbols of love, Blake's thought now turns to
a garden as the place where love would be naturally found; but
the garden where he had played in a state of Innocence is now
occupied by the Chapel of negation, surrounded by the graves of
the instincts. The priest of organized religion is the agent of
repression, and in the illustration he is seen instructing a boy and
a girl in his doctrines. Below, the grave-mound of 'joys and
desires' is seen bound with briars.

Pl. 45   THE LITTLE VAGABOND

The little vagabond, living in the world of Experience, describes
very plainly his naïve notion of an ideal existence with parson
and schoolmistress transformed into figures of benevolence. In the
circumstances he imagines God as a loving father, and the
illustration above is an image of divine forgiveness, the light
around the Godhead dispelling the gloom of the forest of material-
ism and Experience. In the scene below, a family of father,
mother and three children are warming themselves at a blazing
fire.

In the first typographical edition of the *Songs*, published in
1839, this poem was thought too subversive of authority and
was omitted.

Pl. 46   LONDON

The 'mind-forged manacles' of the second stanza shew that in
this poem Blake is writing of a mental state symbolized by the
social injustices seen every day in London. It is a political poem,
the term 'charter'd' applied to the streets and the Thames
signifying the restricting effects of the charters and corporations
of the business world upon the individual. Again, the chimney
sweeper's 'weep, weep' is called upon to illustrate social evils
condoned by the Church, and the soldier's unhappy lot is invoked

as an actual stream of blood running down the walls of the State. Lastly, the manacled mind even converts the marriage bed into a sort of Black Maria, or hearse. This poem is one of Blake's most outspoken protests against the evil effect of industrial civilization upon the life of the individual.

In the illustration a child leads an old man on crutches through the streets. This bearded figure may be the creator, Urizen, himself crippled by the conditions he has created. Below, on the right, another little vagabond is warming himself at a fire.

Pl. 47   THE HUMAN ABSTRACT

'The Human Abstract' was named 'The Human Image' in its first form in manuscript. It is therefore the contrary poem to 'The Divine Image' in *Songs of Innocence*. Blake wrote another poem called 'A Divine Image', but its satire was so savage that he did not use it. In the first stanza of 'The Human Abstract' the poet maintains that abstract reasoning is destructive of joy in life, since the attitudes implicit in pity and mercy presuppose the existence of poverty and suffering. The succeeding stanzas shew how false virtues may arise from selfishness, fear and weakness. In the fourth stanza the Tree of Mystery represents the resulting growth of religion, with the priesthood (the Catterpiller and the Fly) feeding on its leaves. The Raven of the fifth stanza is the symbol of the Fear of Death. The last stanza states that Nature does not know of this Tree. It has grown from Experience, or the reasoning powers of the human mind.

The illustration shews Urizen, the creator, himself tangled in the nets of religion. The poem is not, however, to be understood as a denial of all faith. It is a statement of true faith in the divinity of unrepressed human instincts and the holiness of life.

Pl. 48   INFANT SORROW

'Infant Joy' in *Innocence* was a statement of the simple joy of a life newly conceived. 'Infant Sorrow' shews the other side of the coin. The newly born infant has been brought forth in pain and sorrow and soon becomes a 'fiend' hidden in a 'cloud' of earthly life and experience. The second stanza expresses the human being's inevitable acceptance of his fate, though he can still shew his feelings by sulking.

The illustration suggests the infant's unwilling surrender to his mother's arms.

Pl. 49   A POISON TREE

In the manuscript version of this poem it has the ironic title, 'Christian Forbearance'. It shews how the repression of anger can breed malevolence, so that an artist such as Blake may rejoice in the downfall of a former friend who has stolen his ideas. It is, however, written as a warning, not in exultation. It may be read in conjunction with several of the 'Proverbs of Hell' on the evils of repression in *The Marriage of Heaven and Hell*, and the later couplet addressed to Blake's patron, William Hayley, who had not given him the opportunity to speak his mind:

> Thy Friendship oft has made my heart to ake.
> Do be my Enemy for Friendship's sake.

The design below is a literal illustration of the last stanza.

Pl. 50   A LITTLE BOY LOST

In this poem, not in any way contrasted with 'The Little Boy Lost' of *Innocence*, the child is expressing his instinctive attitude to life, self-love being the natural state. By thought a man can only come to venerate an image of the divinity of man in himself. The child likens himself to a little bird picking up crumbs of self-fulfilment dropped from the tables of more experienced

152

people. The natural truth of this infuriates the priest of organized religion and he makes a martyr of the boy, to the admiration of the unthinking onlookers. Naturalism is thus burnt in the boy's person by the fire of religious zeal. In the design below, the boy's parents and family are shewn vainly weeping before the flames. In the right-hand margin are exaggerated sprigs of ivy, the leaves being given a menacing appearance as symbols of vengeance.

In the last line Blake asks, can such things be done in England, his own country? He was himself never 'educated' in a school and would wish that others should not be subjected to the mental deformation caused by interference with the immature mind.

Pl. 51   A LITTLE GIRL LOST

In the introductory stanza Blake addresses this poem to an idealistic 'future Age', when the hypocrisy of his own time has been shed. Ona, perhaps the feminine form of One, an individual, is personified as a 'little girl', though obviously this is only a poetic conception of the feminine principle. In the six stanzas of the poem proper the story of naturalistic love between the sexes is told as a tragedy. The youthful lovers meet, acknowledge their passion in the morning light, and agree to meet again in the quiet of evening. The girl encounters her father, looking like a 'book', embodying the written laws of forbidden pleasures, and is too terrified to plead her cause. The father is conscious only of outrage, having forgotten in old age the joys of young love.

S. T. Coleridge wished that this poem had been omitted, thinking it could be taken too literally ('not for the want of innocence in the poem, but for the probable want of it in many readers'). Yet it has never been misunderstood in this licentious sense, its meaning in its own context being sufficiently plain.

The decoration is simple, being an innocent-looking tree, with a squirrel and a tiny human figure climbing in the branches. Birds are flying around it at all levels.

Pl. 52   TO TIRZAH

In this obscure poem Tirzah, perhaps to be pronounced 'Tearzah', is addressed in the third stanza as 'Thou Mother of my Mortal part', shewing that she is the maker of the physical body. Blake twice quotes the words of Jesus addressed to his mother in the Temple, 'Then what have I to do with thee?', thus stating the psychological fact that a man is not yet adult until he has thrown off his family ties; not until then is he ready to be freed from earthly generation and to escape to spiritual life. The second stanza relates in four lines the story of the fall of man in Paradise and his condemnation to the sleep of life on earth. In the third and fourth stanzas the poet elaborates the idea of the earthly mother's cruelty in limiting his freedom and imprisoning his senses by material bonds, from which only the death of the Saviour can set him free. The mother's name, Tirzah, is derived from *The Song of Solomon* vi.4, and signifies physical beauty, that is, sex.

In the illustration man's natural body is supported by two women, Mother-love and Sex-love, who failed to save him. At his feet is an aged figure offering him a vessel containing the water of life. On his robe is engraved the second half of St. Paul's sentence, I *Corinthians* xv. 44: 'It is sown a natural body; it is raised a spiritual body'.

Pl. 53   THE SCHOOL-BOY

This lovely poem was at first included by Blake among *Songs of Innocence*, and its theme indeed chimes better with these than with *Experience*. It is a sustained protest, registered also in 'A Little Boy Lost', against the destruction of innocence and youthful joy in life by the dreary round in school, where fears and sorrows cause dismay. Self-development had been Blake's own means of education.

In the left-hand margin is an indeterminate plant with a bird taking wing from its summit. On the right are intertwining vines, their loops reminiscent of the decorations on the 'Introduction' to *Innocence*. Three boys are climbing up the stems, and a fourth sits at the top happily reading the book he was unable to enjoy in school. On the ground two boys and a girl are gathering the fruits fallen from the vine.

Pl. 54 THE VOICE OF THE ANCIENT BARD

This short poem, at first placed by Blake among *Songs of Innocence*, recalls the prophetic Bard with whom the 'Introduction' to *Experience* opened. Now, at the conclusion of the sometimes terrifying visions of Experience, he seeks to reassure the 'Youth of delight' that the morning of regeneration is at hand, when the doubts and disputes of mortal life will be dispelled, even though many have fallen on the way. The versification is unusual, the first line having no rhyme and the last three breaking into an irregularity expressive of the stumbling steps they describe.

The illustration of the Bard with his harp and listening youths and maidens needs no explanation.